STUDY GUIDE

The Assurance of Salvation

R.C. Sproul

LIGONIER MINISTRIES
Renew your Mind.
LIGONIER.ORG | 800-435-4343

421 Ligonier Court, Sanford, FL 32771
Email: info@ligonier.org

Printed in China.

1

The Duty of Pursuing Assurance

MESSAGE INTRODUCTION

Presupposed in our Savior's terrifying words during the Sermon on the Mount (Matt. 7:21) was the reality of a glorious throne room of God, the eternal sanctuary of all those who believe in Him, as well as a wretched abyss of torment reserved not just for the powers of darkness but for those who blaspheme against the Triune God, failing to repent in fruit-producing faith. Jesus contends that one could dupe himself or herself with a false assurance. For this reason, every man and woman must commit to the quest for complete confidence of salvation. In this lecture, Dr. R.C. Sproul expounds upon the duty every Christian has to pursue full assurance.

SCRIPTURE READING

Matthew 7:21–23, 12:46–13:9, 18–23

LEARNING OBJECTIVES

1. To understand why the Christian has a duty to pursue full assurance.
2. To be able to articulate what, according to Jesus, is the true mark of a Christian.

QUOTATIONS

Not everyone who says to Me, "Lord, Lord," shall enter the kingdom of heaven, but he who does the will of My Father in heaven.

—Matthew 7:21

As I watch'd the ploughman ploughing,
Or the sower sowing in the fields—or the harvester harvesting,
I saw there too, O life and death, your analogies:
(Life, life is the tillage, and Death is the harvest according.)

—Walt Whitman, from *Leaves of Grass*

LECTURE OUTLINE

I. Jesus, the "feel-good guru?"

a. The Sermon on the Mount, often regarded as an upbeat message about the ideal life, contains one of the most alarming utterances of Christ Jesus: "'Not everyone who says to Me, "Lord, Lord," shall enter the kingdom of heaven, but he who does the will of My Father in heaven.'" (Matt. 7:21).

b. The following exposition of Matthew 7:21–23 drives those who profess faith in Christ to ponder their assurance that that faith is true.

c. Note that Jesus says He *never* knew the individual who feigned communion with Him, which, of course, precludes the notion that the person in question was ever saved.

d. Note also the use of "Lord, Lord" in verse 21. Addresses such as these denote urgency as well as intimacy (cf. Gen. 2:11, 46:2; Ex. 3:4; 2 Sam. 18:33; Ps. 22:1; Mark 15:34; Luke 10:41, 13:34, 22:31; Acts 9:4, etc.).

e. Therefore, the people described in these verses are those who profess a loving feeling for Christ, but are not known by Him, because, after supposedly entering the kingdom, they have not changed in ways that mark the true Christian.

II. Who, then, does "the will of the Father"?

a. The parable of the soils (Matt. 13:1–9) helps us understand the problem introduced at Matthew 7:21, that not everyone who calls on the Lord will enter the kingdom of heaven, that despite millions of professions, not all are genuine.

b. Matthew 12:46–50 sets up the context: The true mother, brother, or sister of Christ Jesus is the one who does the will of the Father.

c. Notice the similarity to the previous text (Matt. 7:21). Who among those who say, "Lord, Lord," will enter the kingdom of heaven? Those who do the will of the Father. What, then, does this look like? Consider the parable.

d. Starting at Matthew 13:18, Jesus explains the parable of the soils allegorically. (Note that the allegory *is* the message of the story, given by Christ Himself, and so parables should not be treated as allegorical indiscriminately.)

e. The word never sinks into some folks, Jesus says in verse 19, as it does, albeit briefly, into those described in verses 20–21. In today's language, these people may run joyfully down the aisle at an evangelistic crusade, but forget about the planted seed (word) almost immediately.

f. Notice that the signs of faith and the lack thereof are *outward*; that is, one receives the word in joy, endures for a while, and then, under the pressures of trials or persecutions, falls away. Faith in others *can be observed* (Matt. 7:16; James 3:12).

g. Leaving the individuals of verse 22 aside for the present (see lecture No. 4, "False Assurance"), we see that those sown on good soil are hearers who understand. God changes the heart (soil) of the hearers, and the hearers become doers producing fruit.
h. To be sure, not everyone produces the same amount—some a hundredfold, another sixty, and another thirty—but each one produces fruit.
i. This clearly goes against a popular yet false doctrine in the church today, summed up in the catch phrase "carnal Christianity," the idea that one can be a Christian without producing any fruit for a lifetime because of a lingering sin, etc.
j. We are not justified by a mere profession of faith in Jesus, for we are more than able to honor Jesus with our lips when in truth our hearts may be far from Him (Isa. 29:13–14; Mark 7:6–7).
k. Only when we are justified by faith alone does a true profession of faith follow. To correct this falsity in the church, we must leave off counting Christians according to signatures on decision cards; rather, the measuring rod must be the clearly revealed standard of God's Word (therefore hindering both libertines and legalists).

STUDY QUESTIONS

1. According to Jesus in Matthew 7:21, everyone who intimately calls on the Lord and is busy with "Christian" work ________.
   a. Must be a Christian
   b. Must be a liar
   c. Is not necessarily a Christian
   d. None of the above

2. Jesus commands the apostates to depart from Him, saying that they are truly workers of lawlessness, and that He ________ knew them.
   a. Always
   b. Partially
   c. Never
   d. Once

3. The use of a double address (e.g. "Lord, Lord") in Hebrew signified urgency and ________.
   a. Antipathy
   b. Admonition
   c. Intimacy
   d. Exasperation

4. Who will enter the kingdom of heaven, according to Jesus in Matthew 7:21 and 12:50? ________
   a. Whoever has a conversion experience
   b. Whoever makes a profession of faith
   c. Whoever does the Father's will
   d. Both a and b

5. How many "seeds" are truly Christian in the parable of the soils? ________
   a. Three
   b. One
   c. Two
   d. Four

6. "Carnal Christianity" refers to the false notion that ________.
   a. One can deny the deity of Christ and still be saved
   b. One can become a Christian and still eat meat
   c. One can be saved while remaining completely fruitless throughout life
   d. One can be saved and live a completely perfect life

7. Which of the following follows from justification by faith? ________
   a. A true profession of faith
   b. Entrance into the kingdom community
   c. Spiritually good deeds
   d. All of the above

BIBLE STUDY

1. Read Matthew 7:15–20. What two verses share the same principle regarding what determines a person's final destiny? What is the principle that will protect an individual against the coming judgment? What other verse in the gospel of Matthew is identical to verse 19? What issue/danger does this address (cf. Matt. 13:37–43, 49–50; 25:31–46)?

2. Continue reading Matthew 7:21–23. Remember that the cry "Lord, Lord" is an emphatic profession of faith, but still falls short of Jesus' expectations of a true disciple. Is this profession insincere or self-deception (cf. Matt. 25:44)? What, then, is the ultimate criterion for entrance into the kingdom of heaven (e.g. note the two ways the apostate falls short)?

3. Read Matthew 24:36; and Luke 10:12 and 17:31. Now read Isaiah 13:6, 9; Ezekiel 3:30; Amos 5:18, 20; and Zephaniah 1:8, 14, 18. What do you gather "in that day" refers to in Matthew 7:22? Who specifically will be the judge on that day, according to Matthew 7:21–23? Who would Jesus' audience have expected to hear would be judge? Describe and discuss Jesus' striking claim. Why is "charismatic" activity no substitute for genuine obedience and a personal relationship with Christ Jesus?

4. Read Matthew 12:48–49 and compare it with 15:3–6. What is the point here, if not disrespect to His mother (cf. Matt. 10:34–37)? Now focus on Matthew 12:50. The "disciples" (v. 49) thus privileged are described in what way? Thinking back on our discussion of Matthew 7:15–23, what is emphasized once again? What is the true touchstone of an authentic relationship with the Lord Jesus Christ? How does this relate to the following parable of the soils?

DISCUSSION QUESTIONS

1. Discuss as a group how Matthew 7:21–23 drives us to pursue assurance. As a thought-provoking impetus, think of ways you have served the church and plug them into verse 22.
2. In consideration of this lecture's discussion of the Sermon on the Mount and the parable of the soils, what are the true marks of an elect person? Discuss as a group the different soils and their impediments (weeds, sun, birds), and what these "conversion experiences" look like in today's society.
3. If someone you know asserted that a person can be a Christian while spending his or her entire life fruitless, how would you respond? Use Scripture to support your answer.

SUGGESTED READING FOR FURTHER STUDY

MacArthur, John. *The Gospel According to Jesus*, pp. 123–33
Parsons, Burk. *Assured by God*, pp. 19–36
Sproul, R.C. *Getting the Gospel Right*, pp. 167–178
________. *Eternal Security* (audio series)

2

Assurance Enhances Sanctification

MESSAGE INTRODUCTION

It is everywhere assumed in Scripture that full assurance does not come without heavy labor, but the resulting riches are excellent indeed. Why, then, is the quest of making our calling and election a certainty so neglected? Given the danger of false security, the need to awaken ourselves to the kind of persuasion that Saint Paul wrote of in his letter to the Romans (8:38–39) is ineffably great, and must be started without delay. This, the apostle Peter instructs, enhances the sanctification of believers. In this lecture, Dr. R.C. Sproul describes the virtue of pursuing assurance, and the way in which Scripture exhorts us to be diligent in our search.

SCRIPTURE READING

Galatians 5:16–6:10; 1 Peter 1:1–2; 2:1–5; 2 Peter 1:1–11

LEARNING OBJECTIVES

1. To understand how to be diligent in the quest for full assurance.
2. To understand how the pursuit of assurance enhances sanctification.

QUOTATIONS

But the fruit of the Spirit is love, joy, peace, longsuffering, kindness, goodness, faithfulness, gentleness, self-control. Against such there is no law.

—Galatians 5:22–23

Therefore, brethren, be even more diligent to make your call and election sure, for if you do these things you will never stumble.

—2 Peter 1:10

Give me my scallop-shell of quiet,
My staff of faith to walk upon,
My scrip of joy, immortal diet,
My bottle of salvation,
My gown of glory, hope's true gage;
And thus I'll take my pilgrimage.

And when the grand twelve-million jury
Of our sins, with direful fury,
Against our souls black verdicts give,
Christ pleads His death, and then we live.

—Sir Walter Raleigh, "His Pilgrimage"

LECTURE OUTLINE

I. Views on the doctrine of assurance:
  a. Roman Catholics: coming to a full assurance is extremely rare—only those saints who are given "special revelation" can know for certain. Such assurance, Catholics argue, is based upon human conjecture, which, being depraved, is not to be trusted. Canon XV of the Council of Trent on justification states, "If any one saith, that a man, who is born again and justified, is bound of faith to believe that he is assuredly in the number of the predestinate: let him be anathema."
  b. Arminians: Daily assurance is the only possibility, since it is possible for a Christian to fall from saving faith. *Sententiae* ("Opinions") IV.iv of the Arminians asserts that "true believers are able to fall through their own fault into shameful and atrocious deeds, to persevere and to die in them; and therefore finally to fall and to perish."
  c. Magisterial Reformers: Not only is a limited, daily assurance possible, a far-reaching, full assurance unto the very hour of death is equally possible. *The Westminster Confession of Faith*, XVIII.i argues that "such as truly believe in the Lord Jesus, and love him in sincerity, endeavouring to walk in all good conscience before him, may in this life be certainly assured that they are in a state of grace."

II. The apostolic mandate: 2 Peter 1:10
  a. Without ambiguity, Saint Peter charges believers to soberly and diligently strive to make their election a certainty.
  b. It follows, therefore, that if we are called, being in a state of grace, then we are indeed able to attain assurance. This certitude, according to Saint Peter, is not to be postponed, but settled in the present. The exhortation is for believers to know their standing in the kingdom, in Christ.
  c. Those who come to Jesus saying, "Lord, Lord," have a false assurance, proof of which can be seen in their fruitlessness (the parable of the soils).
  d. This is not a repudiation of the Protestant doctrine of justification by faith alone. The magisterial Reformers emphasized a *vives fide* (a living faith). True faith *always* manifests itself in good works.

e. Roman Catholics, however, teach that good works combined with faith lead to justification. The Protestant twist on this is, "We are justified by faith alone, but not by a faith that is alone."
f. Do we therefore seek to resolve assurance by examining our fruits? Yes, but we cannot rely totally on this for we all fall far short. In whom or what, according to 2 Timothy 1:12, did Saint Paul place his confidence?
g. The apostle Peter is saying, then, that we are to strive to make our election sure in order to bear fruit—not vice versa, where we might actually root our assurance in the good works themselves (in the parable of the sower in Matt. 13, both the rocky soil and the thorny soil encountered this problem—only the last soil had the freedom to grow). This enhances rather than hinders our sanctification by bringing us into the freedom found only in full assurance.
h. Note the parallels between Saint Peter's list of fruits (2 Peter 1:3–8) and Saint Paul's fruits of the Spirit (Gal. 5:22–23).
i. The apostle Peter's first letter is addressed to "the elect" and focuses on what it means to be the elect during their spiritual journey. This helps to teach us the differences between true and false assurance.
j. In 1 Peter 2:1–5, Saint Peter states plainly that Christ is precious to those who believe in Him. The essential first step in making our election sure, then, is determining what we think of the person, Jesus.

STUDY QUESTIONS

1. Roman Catholics and Arminians essentially agree that ________.
   a. Daily assurance of salvation is quite possible
   b. Full assurance of salvation in this life is nearly impossible
   c. Those whom God has predestined will be preserved until the end
   d. Both a and b

2. Which of the following best articulates the substance of 2 Peter 1:10? ________
   a. The apostle is commanding believers to base their election and assurance on the good works they should be performing.
   b. The apostle, knowing that full assurance is an impossibility, makes the call anyway in order to promote good deeds.
   c. The apostle exhorts believers to make their election sure, and fully expects them to be capable of doing so.
   d. None of the above

3. The magisterial Reformers emphasized a *vives fide*, a "living faith" that ________.
   a. Is really no different than the Roman Catholic view of justification
   b. Always manifests itself in good works
   c. Does not necessarily manifest itself in good works
   d. Conjoins good works and faith, thereby producing salvation

4. In what do we place our ultimate confidence when seeking full assurance once we have believed in the Gospel? ________
   a. The examination of our works
   b. Jesus' keeping what we have committed to Him until that Day
   c. Our personal piety
   d. Our ability to understand and teach the Word of God

5. Striving to make our election sure, according to Saint Peter, ________.
   a. Is to be postponed, since we cannot be certain of it anyway
   b. Rests solely on our producing fruit
   c. Enhances our sanctification
   d. Is futile

6. What does 2 Peter share (among other things) with Saint Paul's epistle to the Galatians? ________
   a. Length
   b. A list of fruits
   c. Literary structure
   d. A gospel narrative

7. To those who believe, according to 1 Peter 2:1–5, Jesus is seen as ________.
   a. A rock of offense
   b. A stone of stumbling
   c. The lamb
   d. Precious

BIBLE STUDY

1. Read 2 Peter 1:10. Does this verse mean that the call and election of God is uncertain in itself? If not, what does it imply? What things must we do, according to Saint Peter, so that we "will never stumble"? Do these good works give us faith or strengthen our faith? Are these fruits of faith a result of physical power or spiritual power? Which one, in the end, increases the more a person makes use of it and applies it (cf. Ps. 46:10; Gal. 6:8)?
2. Read Ecclesiastes 9:10. If the Preacher exhorts us to be diligent in matters of the flesh, how much more should we be in matters of the spirit? Discuss ways in which this can be done. Continue with Hebrews 12:15. What is the explicit possibility delineated in this verse? How do the five foolish virgins of Matthew 25 relate to this passage from Hebrews (cf. Luke 13:23–27)?
3. Read 1 Peter 5:8 (cf. Matt. 23:15; Eph. 4:14). Striving to make our election sure, in light of these passages, becomes even more urgent. Why? Read Habakkuk 2:12–13, Micah 7:3, and Jeremiah 23:10. How are non-believers described in these

passages? Are we Christians just as diligent in our endeavor as the unregenerate person who is literally running to get into hell? Discuss this last question as a group.

4. Read 2 Peter 3:14, then Isaiah 32:17. How does being diligent in this matter enhance our sanctification, according to these passages? Read 1 Corinthians 15:58. What can we be assured of, if we have been assiduous in producing fruit? If we have not, given the urgency of the issue (our very salvation!), what are we waiting for?

DISCUSSION QUESTIONS

1. Suppose you have a friend who disdains the idea of full assurance, saying that it is quite impossible unless you are especially pious, holy, etc. How would you respond? Suppose that friend is unsaved. How then would you respond?
2. What if a Christian friend objected to full assurance on the grounds that many people wrongly boast of their salvation and perish. What would your answer be? Use Scripture to support your response. Must a balance be struck between a grandiose triumphalism and a somber melancholy? Why or why not? Which one do you tend toward?
3. Discuss as a group the various ways in which God confirms His salvation in your life. Be specific, and do not restrict your answers to just one facet of God's revelation—that is, show how the entire sphere of God's revelation works to bolster your assurance of salvation.

SUGGESTED READING FOR FURTHER STUDY

Love, Christopher. *A Treatise of Effectual Calling and Election*

Spurgeon, C.H. "Full Assurance," *Free Grace Broadcaster*, (Issue 179, Winter 2002).

3

Four Kinds of People

MESSAGE INTRODUCTION

The world is filled with as many opinions as there are people. Even within the smallest minority, disagreement is bound to exist. One thing, however, unifies certain individuals and separates them from the world at large—their relationship with the living God. Still, not all people are sure about their standing in this relationship with Him. To be sure, many do know that they are saved or unsaved, but there are just as many who are unknowingly saved as there are those who fool themselves into thinking they are saved. In this lecture, Dr. R.C. Sproul explains how each of these categories represents assurance and how they relate to the Christian's quest of making his or her election certain.

SCRIPTURE READING

Romans 1:18–25; Hebrew 6:10–12; Ephesians 4:13–14; Matthew 19:16–22

LEARNING OBJECTIVES

To be able to explain what each of the four kinds of people believe regarding the assurance of salvation.

QUOTATIONS

Although the time of death is approaching me, I am not afraid of dying and going to Hell or (what would be considerably worse) going to the popularized version of Heaven. I expect death to be nothingness, and, for removing me from all possible fears of death, I am thankful to atheism.

—Isaac Asimov

Nevertheless I am not ashamed, for I know whom I have believed and am persuaded that He is able to keep what I have committed to Him until that Day.

—2 Timothy 1:12

HONEST: Difficulties, lions, or Vanity Fair, [Mr. Fearing] feared not at all; it was only sin, death, and hell, that were to him a terror, because he had some doubts about his interest in that celestial country.

—John Bunyan, *Pilgrim's Progress*

Many will say to Me in that day, "Lord, Lord, have we not prophesied in Your name, cast out demons in Your name, and done many wonders in Your name?" And then I will declare to them, "I never knew you; depart from Me, you who practice lawlessness!"

—Matthew 7:22–23

LECTURE OUTLINE

I. First person: unsaved and knows it
  a. These people are unflinchingly godless and know where this leads.
  b. Romans 1: Saint Paul says that through the revelation of God in nature people know (via conscience) that they are in rebellion against their Creator ("who by their unrighteousness suppress the truth . . . for His eternal power and divine nature have been clearly perceived, ever since the creation of the world, in the things that have been made" [Rom. 1:18, 20]).
  c. Lying beneath the surface is an awareness of this abysmal rift and rebellion ("The wicked flee when no one pursues . . ." [Prov. 28:1]).
  d. Many in this group attempt the "foxhole conversion"—living a godless life until the very end and then looking for the loopholes.

II. Second person: saved and knows it
  a. It is possible by way of Scripture and the inner testimony of the Holy Spirit to gain full assurance (see lectures 5–6)

III. Third person: saved and knows it not
  a. It is quite possible to be in a state of grace while being unaware of that fact (2 Peter 1:10 presupposes this).
  b. Some challenge this, however, saying that saving faith must entail cognizant confidence in one's salvation.
    i. While some people can recall the day, hour, and minute of their conversion, many who have been reared in the faith cannot (and should not) narrow the moment of conversion down in this manner.
    ii. We must be wary of elevating our personal experiences into normative standards. Such practices lead to a false assurance, and are fostered by

the American "revival" mentality, whereby "conversion experiences" are not distinguished from true "conversions."

c. It is important to remember that nobody is half-regenerated by the Holy Spirit. Redemption is applied fully and instantly by the power of God.
d. The normative standard for faith and practice is the Word of God, and so our experiences and assurance must be tested therein. One of the most dangerous things we can do as Christians is to base our theology on personal experiences without first subjecting them to the Holy Scriptures.

IV. Fourth person: unsaved yet assured of salvation

a. These people are much more complicated to explain, since they exude confidence that they are saved.
b. It is just as important for us to recognize the counterfeit as it is to recognize the genuine. The more we understand their differences, the better able we are to discover the charlatan.
c. Ironically, the church throughout history has been aided by heresy, for many essential doctrines have been solidified while combatting it. The church is often forced in such times to examine the truth more carefully.
d. The confidence with which this group acts produces the tension that we are trying to resolve in our quest for full assurance. The question we face when comparing persons two and four is: "I have assurance, but how can I be sure of this assurance? Am I sure that I am sure?"
e. Answers to the question of full assurance fall on a long continuum, as seen in the idea of certainty, and how it can be represented in various degrees. This accentuates what is the norm for human confidence—vacillation.
f. The search for assurance, then, rests on the possibility of finding a solid foundation on which we can build.

STUDY QUESTIONS

1. The first person described in this lecture truly knows of his or her rebellion. What portion of Scripture best articulates this position? ________
   a. James 2
   b. Habakkuk 2
   c. Romans 1
   d. All of the above

2. Which of the following Scripture passages best represents this person's attitude toward God? ________
   a. 1 Peter 2:7a
   b. Psalm 48:9–11
   c. Romans 8:7
   d. Matthew 5:3–12

3. Those in the second category, those who are saved and know it, gain true assurance through the following combination of which two? ________
    a. Church membership and frequency of ministry-related service
    b. Tithing and participation in the sacraments
    c. Fervent prayer and the "fact" that all persons will be saved
    d. The Scriptures and the inner testimony of the Spirit

4. Among many other Scripture passages that exhort us to establish a firm hope in Christ Jesus, 2 Peter 1:10 also presupposes ________.
    a. That all believers will have full assurance
    b. That a believer may never arrive at an assured hope
    c. That one cannot be saved and have a lack of assurance
    d. That a person can be in a state of grace and yet not be fully saved

5. The idea of "conversion experience" might correspond with which of the following seeds from the parable of the soils (Matt. 13:1–23)? ________
    a. The seeds fallen by the wayside
    b. The seeds fallen on stony places
    c. The seeds fallen among thorns
    d. Both b and c

6. Throughout Christendom, the universal church has been aided by ________ when solidifying sound doctrine.
    a. Various calibers of churchmen-theologians
    b. Heresies
    c. The Holy Spirit
    d. All of the above

7. The more able we are to recognize and understand counterfeit conversions, the better able we are to ________.
    a. Discover the validity of our own faith
    b. Pinpoint the charlatan
    c. Articulate the true Gospel
    d. All of the above

BIBLE STUDY

1. Read Matthew 12:20 and 17:20, and John 6:37. What do these verses say about both the quantity and quality of faith? Is faith measured by its degree or its verity? Read Romans 10:11. What must the Christian do in order to be saved? Does justification or sanctification work itself out in degrees? Discuss this as a group.

2. Can you find where a strong and mighty faith is guaranteed in Scripture? Are there any distinctions to be made between faith and assurance? Why or why not? Read Matthew 14:30 and Acts 4:11–12, then Acts 9:11 and 2 Timothy 1:12 and 4:8. Describe what changes, if any, took place in these men.
3. Read Acts 8:1–3 and 9:1–30. Contemplate this story of conversion. What are some of the ways in which you lack the assurance of your salvation? How could this event in the book of Acts reveal God's mercy and provide the doubting Christian with peace?

DISCUSSION QUESTIONS

1. Doubt strikes us all. Discuss as a group how the following can lead to it: 1) disobedience; 2) spiritual immaturity; 3) emotional exhaustion; 4) strong conviction; 5) certain sins deemed "unforgivable"; 6) misinterpretation of Scripture; 7) failure to recall the "exact moment" of conversion. Can you name and describe any more?
2. Suppose a friend fears for his salvation and feels himself hardening to the means of grace and the things of God. What Scripture passages could you use to comfort him? What practical observations (i.e. applied Scripture) could you make to help guide him?
3. Read Psalm 46:10 and discuss as a group how this teaching differs from the popular phrase "Let go, and let God." How does this passage in the Psalms relate to the quest for full assurance? That is, what does it mean to "be still" or "cease striving?"
4. How is it that a person can be intently focused on his or her sin, constantly mourning over it, and yet receive little or no remedy? Read Matthew 13:44–45. If faith is the buying of the field or the merchant's search, then what is the actual treasure or pearl of great price? What, then, is absolutely necessary for the obtaining of full assurance? Is the faith described here a "blind leap"? Why or why not?

SUGGESTED READING FOR FURTHER STUDY

Hooker, Thomas. *The Poor Doubting Christian Drawn to Christ*
Ryle, J.C. "Assurance," *Holiness*, pp. 119–160
Sproul, R.C. *Guilt and Forgiveness* (audio series)

4

False Assurance

MESSAGE INTRODUCTION

Living the lie of feigned obedience to the Lord is one of the saddest, most enigmatic displays of man's depravity. The apostate who works within the walls of Christianity—the faithless minister who seeks nothing but power, the evangelist who seeks nothing but glory, the philanthropist who seeks to assuage self-loathing—leads a life of seeming faith, but in the end finds himself or herself unknown by Christ Jesus. What fosters such a lie in the individual? In this lesson, Dr. R.C. Sproul seeks to answer this perplexing question by discussing the errors that lead to a life of false assurance.

SCRIPTURE READING

Matthew 19:16–20:16

LEARNING OBJECTIVES

1. To understand and articulate the requirements of salvation, that is, to defend a Biblically sound soteriology (doctrine of salvation).
2. To be able to explain the various errors that lead to a false assurance.

QUOTATIONS

The young man said to Him, "All these things I have kept from my youth. What do I still lack?"

—Matthew 19:20

To me the gentle guide: "Inquirest thou not what spirits
Are these which thou beholdest? Ere thou pass
Farther, I would thou know, that these of sin
Were blameless; and if aught they merited,

It profits not, since baptism was not theirs,
The portal to thy faith."

"O tell me, sire revered!
Tell me, my master!" I began, through wish
Of full assurance in that holy faith
Which vanquishes all error; "say, did e'er
Any, or through his own or other's merit,
Come forth from thence, who afterward was blest?"

—Dante Alighieri, *Inferno*, Canto IV

LECTURE OUTLINE

I. The fourth person revisited
  a. This category, or type of person, complicates the question of full assurance, and demands that those who are assured of their salvation ask the question, "What, then, leads to a false assurance?"
  b. There are two reasons behind the major errors that lead to false assurance:
    i. The falsely assured do not understand what salvation entails (i.e., they lack a sound soteriology).
    ii. Or, while understanding a distinctly Biblical soteriology, they have not truly met the requirements of salvation.

II. Major errors that lead to a false assurance
  a. *Universalism*—an anti-Biblical doctrine of salvation. Regarding false assurance, it can be summed up in the following proposition: "If every person is saved, and I am a person, then I am assured of my salvation."
    i. Universalism is one of the most prevalent views of salvation outside of Christianity, as seen in the common answer to the question, "How do you get to heaven?" "That's simple," many would say, "the answer is 'die'." We have all but eradicated any notion of divine wrath in this current age.
    ii. Scripture warns, however, that "it is appointed for men to die once, but after this the judgment" (Heb. 9:27). And Jesus, contrary to popular opinion, spoke about hell and judgment more than any "fire-and-brimstone" evangelist (or for that matter, more than any other figure in Scripture).
  b. *Legalism* (works-righteousness)—yet another anti-Biblical doctrine of salvation whereby entrance into heaven rests squarely upon one's strict adherence to the law of God.
    i. Legalism is also one of the most widespread soteriologies, given that many people answer the question, "How do you get to heaven?" by saying "I'm not perfect, but I've lived a good life."

ii. This is counterfeit assurance, as well, for Saint Paul writes, "for by the works of the law no flesh shall be justified" (Gal. 2:16).

iii. Consider the story of the rich young ruler (Matt. 19:16–22). In response to being called "good," Jesus says, in effect: "Your understanding of 'good' is superficial. Haven't you read the Psalms? No one is good except God" (cf. Rom. 3:10–18, and take note of the many cross references).

iv. The idea of good can be judged in two ways: 1) Unknowing obedience to the law of God, also known as a "civic fair dealing and order" (cf. Calvin's Institutes, 2.2.12–17). This describes the pagan who engages in civic virtue. 2) Obedience to the law of God that flows from a desire for God—otherwise known as "Christian virtue."

v. An adept teacher (surely the best), Jesus chooses not to rail the young financier about his depravity; rather He simply challenges the man's supposed legalistic purity with the very first commandment of the Decalogue: "You shall have no other gods before Me" (Deut. 5:7).

vi. "If you want to be perfect, go, sell what you have and give to the poor . . . " (Matt. 19:21). And the man went away sorrowful, exposed, for his god was riches, and to part with them would have been like parting with himself.

vii. Jesus, of course, was not suggesting a different way to salvation; rather He was challenging the common assumption that we are the best judges of our own righteousness (cf. 2 Cor. 10:12, where Saint Paul writes of the unwise judges who measure themselves by themselves).

c. *Sacerdotalism*—salvation, according to this error, comes by way of the sacraments (see quote from Dante above). The Pharisees suffered from this view, thinking that their circumcision automatically included them in the kingdom of God. In like manner, one can think membership in the visible church means membership in the invisible church. Trusting in these outward signs alone leads to a false assurance.

i. Examples of sacerdotalism are found in evangelicalism. For example, the "sinner's prayer," going forward during an altar call, or making a decision and signing the card, while not inherently wrong, can (and often do) lead to a sense of assurance that is false, putting hope in the *act* of coming to Jesus rather than in the crucified Christ.

STUDY QUESTIONS

1. The word *soteriology* refers to ________.
   a. The doctrine of the Holy Spirit
   b. The doctrine of salvation
   c. The "doctrines of grace"
   d. The doctrine of the soul

2. Which of the following theological systems is a major error that leads to a false assurance? ________
   a. Legalism
   b. Calvinism
   c. Universalism
   d. Both a and c

3. Universalism is a doctrine of salvation that teaches ________.
   a. Christ's atonement is sufficient for all, but efficient only for the elect
   b. God elects some, not all, of humanity to glorify His name forever
   c. All of humanity will be restored on the Last Day
   d. The human soul will cease to exist upon the death of the body

4. Legalism can best be summed up as ________.
   a. A doctrine of salvation whereby entrance into heaven rests upon the grace of God
   b. A doctrine of salvation whereby entrance into heaven rests upon one's confession that Jesus is Lord and belief that He was raised from the dead
   c. A doctrine of salvation whereby entrance into heaven rests upon one's justification by faith
   d. A doctrine of salvation whereby entrance into heaven rests squarely upon one's strict adherence to the law of God

5. Legalists measure their own righteousness ________.
   a. With the Word of God
   b. Partly through the attestations of other believers
   c. With themselves
   d. Through the inner testimony of the Spirit

6. "Trusting solely in the outward signs of the church for salvation" best describes which false soteriology? ________
   a. Universalism
   b. Sacerdotalism
   c. Legalism
   d. None of the above

7. Sacerdotalism is portrayed in which of the following ways? ________
   a. Pharisees who believed themselves to be a part of the kingdom automatically via circumcision
   b. Thinking that being a member of the visible church means being a member of the invisible church, as well
   c. Grounding one's assurance in the act of saying the "sinner's prayer"
   d. All of the above

BIBLE STUDY

1. Read James 4:1–10. Describe in today's terminology the one who ignores a life of repentance. What might true repentance look like (v. 9)? Read Hebrews 6:4–12. What is the author teaching us in this passage about a life of repentance versus the life of one who has fallen away? Now read Hebrews 12:16–17. Why was Esau's repentance false? Have you ever confessed with insincere motives? How can the Christian avoid such callousness?
2. Contemplate Romans 8:5–17. Make two lists. In list one, write down the characteristics of the non-believer; in the second list, the attributes of the believer. What are some of the main differences? How does this challenge or confirm your faith?
3. In our lecture today, the rich young ruler was exposed as a legalist—one who judged his own righteousness with himself as the standard. It seems Jesus demands the impossible here, that is, perfect obedience to the law of God. With which commandment would Jesus challenge you? What would you say if asked what one must do to inherit eternal life?
4. Read Mark 10:24–27. How does this passage help us understand what it means to be perfect, as Christ Himself is perfect? How does it provide comfort and assurance? How might it unsettle the legalist?

DISCUSSION QUESTIONS

1. Suppose you have a friend whose faith is questionable. While you are exhorting her unto true repentance, she responds, "But I am very emotional when I pray, and sometimes I see my prayers answered. Is this not a sign of faith?" Discuss your response as a group using Scripture.
2. What if that same friend is the busiest of persons, attending Bible studies, choir practices, evangelism outreaches, etc. Suppose she points to her enthusiastic service as proof of her Christianity. How would you respond? Can you think of any persons portrayed in Scripture who also fit this description?
3. Is the popular slogan, "Once saved, always saved," the best way to summarize an assurance of salvation? Why or why not? In what ways might it undermine a Biblical view of sanctification (or repentance)? How does it conflict, if at all, with 2 Peter 1:10? Discuss as a group the struggles and lack of assurance we face at various times. Which is better—to face doubt or to never think about it?

SUGGESTED READING FOR FURTHER STUDY

Mead, Matthew. *The Almost Christian Discovered*
Pink, Arthur W. *The Christian in Romans 7*
Ryle, J.C. "Holiness," *Holiness*, pp. 41–118

5

Gaining True Assurance

MESSAGE INTRODUCTION

We saw earlier in this series that many people within the wide realm of evangelicalism believe that full assurance is wishful thinking. Some think it entirely unfitting for the Christian to pursue; others think daily assurance is as far as one can get. Much of this has to do with a non-Reformed understanding of the doctrine of perseverance—the belief that those with saving faith can indeed fall away. Given that none of us knows what the future holds, can we really say with certainty that we are saved from all eternity into all eternity? Answering in the affirmative, Dr. R.C. Sproul explains in this lesson what the Scriptures say regarding the possibility of gaining true assurance.

SCRIPTURE READING

John 17:6–26; Romans 8:28–39

LEARNING OBJECTIVES

1. To be able to summarize the various views on predestination and how they affect the doctrine of assurance.
2. To understand the relationship between the Reformed doctrine of election and full assurance.

QUOTATIONS

Ho! Everyone who thirsts, come to the waters; and you who have no money, come, buy and eat. Yes, come, buy wine and milk without money and without price.

—Isaiah 55:1

. . . for I am past

All fearing now. But Fate may send a fly
Sometimes, and he may sting us to the grave.
So driven to test our faith in what we see.

—Edwin Arlington Robinson, "Merlin," VII

LECTURE OUTLINE

I. How do we gain a true assurance?

a. If false assurance is a sure result of false doctrines of salvation, then a Biblical expression of both election and soteriology must be understood in order to make our election sure (2 Peter 1:10).

b. An anti-Biblical doctrine of election will certainly lead to an anti-Biblical doctrine of salvation. Though we can distinguish between them, we cannot separate them—they are inextricably tied together.

II. Two opposing views of election

a. Prescient predestination: According to this view, election unto salvation is a result of our believing in Christ—which believing has been foreseen by God before the foundation of the world. The result of God's foreseeing, then, is our election. Salvation ultimately rests upon that one, fateful decision at that point and time we are faced with the Gospel of Christ Jesus. (Prescient predestinarians historically have struggled to gain true assurance as a result of their performance-driven theology.)

b. Biblical election: According to this view, election *is* unto salvation. God calls His people and they come, because they have been elected before the foundation of the world. None of those who are not saved are a part of the elect. Contrarily, those who are saved are of the elect.

i. In His "High-Priestly Prayer"(John 17:6ff), Jesus prays specifically for His disciples, as well as those who will believe in Him through their word (John 17:20).

ii. One major point in this prayer is Jesus' affirmation that all who come to Him have been given to the Son by the Father, and not one of them is lost (John 17:12).

iii. This, then, forces us to ask, "Are we numbered among the elect?" If I am sure that I am elect, then I can be sure of my salvation. God's purpose for the elect, as revealed in Scripture, is to save them.

III. On to assurance via the *ordo salutis*

a. The order of salvation, or *ordo salutis*, is not to be viewed as a temporal chain of events, but a logical one. For example, when we come to saving faith, we are instantaneously justified. Yet faith precedes justification logically (not in time) because faith is the necessary prerequisite for justification (cf. Gal. 3:24).

b. The so-called "golden chain" of Romans 8:28ff provides us with a better understanding of how the elect can be assured of their salvation. This chain, however, is an abbreviated *ordo salutis* that only highlights the Christian journey.

c. Romans 8:28—the "call" in view here is a special, particular calling. There is certainly a general calling for every person to confess that Jesus Christ is Lord, but the calling of verse 28 is effective while the general call to repent is not. Many reject the outer call, but the inward call of God accomplishes that which He intends—eternal salvation.
d. That the "called" of verse 28 are the elect is clearly proved by looking at the elliptical nature of the "golden chain." For example, in verses 29–30, all who are predestined are foreknown, all who are called are predestined, and all who are justified are called (and predestined and foreknown, etc.). This precludes the notion that this calling is an ineffectual, general command.
e. Remember that prescient predestinarians regard foreknowledge as the basis for God's election of people, and they use this text to support their claim. Romans 9, however, challenges and defeats this pretension (cf. Rom. 9:11).
f. Reformed Christians contend, contrary to prescient predestinarians, that the people elected by God are not nameless ciphers (non-entities), but are specific, foreknown individuals (implying intimate personal relationships, not mere awareness of facts and circumstances).

IV. If being called means being justified, how do we know we are of the called?

a. Ephesians 2:1ff—If you have been quickened ("you who were *made alive*, who were dead in trespasses and sins"), then you are of the elect.
b. The apostle Paul in this passage focuses on the grace of God and regeneration of the soul, a quickening that leads into conformity with God's character (v. 10).
c. Being certain of our election, or calling, then, is univocal with eternal salvation. Despite the massive confusion today among evangelicals regarding regeneration (and subsequently assurance), the Christian can walk with confidence, saying, "I know whom I have believed. . . . There is laid up for me the crown of righteousness" (2 Tim. 1:12; 4:8).

STUDY QUESTIONS

1. The relationship between soteriology and any doctrine of election is ________.
   a. Indistinguishable. They are one and the same
   b. Loosely connected. Certain views of election may or may not influence one's doctrine of salvation
   c. Non-existent. Whatever one believes regarding election makes no impact on one's doctrine of salvation
   d. Inextricable. One's view of election will influence one's view of salvation

2. Prescient predestinarians believe which of the following? ________

a. That God commands all to repent, but elects a particular number of people
b. That God, in His sovereignty, elects every person ever created
c. That God elects people based on His foreknowledge that they will choose Him
d. None of the above

3. In the "High-Priestly Prayer" Jesus prays ________.
   a. For Himself
   b. For the whole world
   c. For the twelve disciples only
   d. For those whom the Father has given Him

4. Regarding assurance, being a part of the elect means ________.
   a. That we can know that we are saved, but only day to day
   b. Being saved from all eternity into all eternity
   c. Nothing at all in relation to salvation
   d. One can sin as much as he or she wants

5. Which of the following best describes the *ordo salutis*? ________
   a. It is a prime example of how Aristotelian philosophy influenced the apostle Paul.
   b. It is a rigid temporal sequence of events describing the order of salvation.
   c. It is a logical sequence of events to be taken holistically as a description of our salvation.
   d. None of the above

6. Who are the "called" in Romans 8:28? ________
   a. The non-elect
   b. The elect
   c. The whole world
   d. Members of the Presbyterian Church

7. If being inwardly called is univocal with being justified, what is one sign of this quickening, according to Ephesians 2:10? ________
   a. Hatred of all believers who fall into sin
   b. Disdain for all organized Christian religion
   c. Conforming to the image of Christ Jesus through good works
   d. Listening to contemporary Christian music

BIBLE STUDY

1. Read 1 John 3:11–24. How does this passage help us understand whether we are saved or not? What does it say regarding assurance? Continue with 1 John 4:7–21. What, according to these verses, does the believer look like? How does this passage relate to our discussion of assurance? How do both of these passages reinforce the apostle Peter's call to strive to make our election sure?
2. Read John 17:6–26. What does this text say about the relationship between election and assurance? How does it contribute to our understanding of the doctrine of sanctification?
3. As 1 John 4:12–21 states, believers know that they abide in God because He has given them the Spirit, they confess that Jesus is the Son of God, they abide in and believe in the love that God has for them, and they show that love to their "brothers." Read Romans 8:28–30. How does this chain, taken as a whole unit, emphasize this abiding in, or union with, the Trinity? That is, what does it mean that believers are "predestined to be conformed to the image of his Son, in order that he might be the firstborn among many brothers"?
4. What event holds pre-eminence in this passage (Rom. 8:28) by serving as the grounds of both our salvation and assurance (cf. Rom. 6:4; 1 Thess. 4:14, 16; 1 Cor. 15:22–23; Col. 1:15, 18)? How do these passages help us better understand the so-called "golden chain" of Romans 8:28–30? Can you think of any similitudes or analogies in Scripture of this mystical union that help accentuate its nature?

DISCUSSION QUESTIONS

1. In your own words, compare and contrast the differing views on predestination and how they relate to the doctrine of assurance. Which view is the most conducive to obtaining full assurance? Elaborate.
2. Using Scripture, defend the Reformed view of election from those who argue that God predestines according to His prescience. Now do the opposite: Defend prescient predestination from the Reformed view. Which one finds the least plausibility according to the plain sense of the Scriptures?
3. Living a life of repentance is essential to our sanctification. Disingenuous confession, however, will have adverse affects on our assurance. What are some ways we can keep our motivations pure?
4. Discuss as a group the "already/not yet" character of the "golden chain" in Romans 8:28–30.

SUGGESTED READING FOR FURTHER STUDY

Love, Christopher. *A Treatise of Effectual Calling and Election*
Ryle, J.C. "Sanctification," *Holiness*, pp. 19–40

6

The Source of Full Assurance

MESSAGE INTRODUCTION

"Now faith is the assurance of things hoped for, the conviction of things not seen" (Heb. 11:1). Faith, the author of Hebrews writes, is necessary in gaining true assurance. But what empowers such faith? That which is the very source of the Christian's unwavering, sanctified assurance in the salvation of Christ Jesus. But, as we have seen in earlier lectures, many people are confused about what exactly the supreme source of assurance is. In this final lesson, Dr. R.C. Sproul teaches that Holy Writ, coupled with the testimony of the Holy Spirit, serves as the only true ground upon which Christians can base their hope in eternal salvation.

SCRIPTURE READING

2 Corinthians 1:15–22; 5:1–11; Romans 8:1–17

LEARNING OBJECTIVES

1. To understand one of the Holy Spirit's major roles in salvation—restoring the image of God in the believer.
2. To be able to correct prevalent false views about regeneration (e.g. "carnal Christianity," etc.).

QUOTATIONS

Lay down a pledge for me with yourself; who is there who will put up security for me?

. . . Where then is my hope? Who will see my hope? Will it go down to the bars of Sheol? Shall we descend together in the dust?

—Job 17:3, 15–16

When, God knows, I'm toss'd about
Either with despair or doubt;
Yet before the glass be out,
Sweet Spirit, comfort me!

When the tempter me pursu'th
With the sins of all my youth,
And half damns me with untruth,
Sweet Spirit, comfort me!

—Robert Herrick, "Litany to the Holy Spirit"

LECTURE OUTLINE

I. What does "quickening" have to do with a sound soteriology?
   a. A good theology of salvation begins with a Biblical understanding of the Holy Spirit's role in redemption. Being born again is not primarily about the act of coming to Christ ("sinner's prayer," etc.). It first and foremost has to do with the regenerating work of the Spirit in the life of the believer—a work that effects a change.
   b. This quickening wrought by the Holy Spirit raises us from death to life. The state of our souls in original sin is not sickness, but death itself. The Spirit works to resurrect our corrupted image and restore it for God's glory.
   c. Much confusion, however, has arisen over the centuries regarding the depths of our depravity. Some believe that the fall of man was partial, that a little righteousness remained so as to enable us to choose to obey Jesus by the Spirit's universal grace. But the Biblical portrayal of the Fall is total:
      i. The unregenerate person manifestly hates God in both word and deed, heart and actions (Rom. 3:9–20).
      ii. The soul has an inclination or disposition that, prior to regeneration, is entirely antipathetic toward God (cf. 1 Kings 8:46; Rom. 8:7; Eph. 2:1).
   d. There are three questions one might ask to judge if this quickening has taken place:
      i. Do you love Christ Jesus perfectly?
      ii. Do you love Christ Jesus as much as you ought?
      iii. Do you love the Biblical Christ at all? (with an emphasis on "biblical," since many people are converted to a false idea of the Christ of Christianity).
   e. It is quite impossible for an unregenerate person to have any affection for Jesus as Lord and Savior, for this is precisely what the regenerating power of the Holy Spirit imparts. Therefore, answering "yes" to question iii. above carries with it a signal of salvation (though not definitive).
   f. Notice how this counteracts the false view of regeneration that asserts the Spirit's sanctifying work depends solely on a person's decision to be filled with God's grace. This opens the possibility that a completely unfruitful Christian can exist. But how can a person be transformed inwardly if outwardly he or she remains unchanged?

II. Further attestations of the Word and Spirit

a. 2 Corinthians 5:1–6. Paul here speaks of the Spirit as a *"pledge"* (v.5, Greek: *arrhabon*), language used in the marketplace of his day. He conveys the idea that when we become regenerated, the Father is giving us the Spirit as an earnest, or down payment, that ensures full payment (the fullness of salvation realized).

b. 2 Corinthians 1:15–22. This passage essentially speaks of the promises of God as neither vacillating nor ambiguous. His covenant is firmly established by divine affirmation. And it goes even further. We have actually been sealed by and given "the Spirit in our hearts as a pledge" (v. 22, same word as above; cf. Job 17:3), an infallible and indelible mark and testimony.

c. Romans 8:9. While we seek to examine our fruit and test it against the Scriptures, in the end assurance rests on that promise confirmed in the Word that the Spirit, without whom one cannot be saved, bears witness to our spirit.

d. We know that that which fills us is the Spirit of God because the Word of God confesses this for our sakes. The key is becoming saturated with Him. The more deluged we become, the more we grow in the faith, His Spirit attesting to the spirit within us. Our works, therefore, become increasingly sanctified, which leads to a greater assurance of our election unto salvation.

STUDY QUESTIONS

1. The Bible portrays sin as ________ as opposed to ________.
   a. Sickness, death
   b. A minor behavioral fault, a moral failure
   c. Fulfilling, unfulfilling
   d. Death, sickness

2. The image of God (*imago Dei*) has been ________.
   a. Completely lost by the fall of man into sin
   b. Partially tainted by the Fall, leaving man with the ability to pine after God
   c. Corrupted by the Fall, though man is still not as evil as possible
   d. None of the above

3. The human soul's natural disposition toward God is best described in which of the following ways? ________
   a. Sometimes hatred, sometimes love
   b. Animosity
   c. Love
   d. Indifference, neutrality

4. The Holy Spirit's regenerating work in individuals depends ________.
   a. Pre-eminently on human decisions
   b. On God's capricious choice

c. Upon the reception of baptism or not
d. On God's sovereign grace

5. Which of the following best describes the "Spirit as guarantee" (2 Cor. 5:5)? ________
   a. The Holy Spirit is a guarantee for daily faith, but offers no assurance
   b. While the Holy Spirit is not imparted, a promise is nonetheless given
   c. The Holy Spirit is a down payment on a future glory
   d. None of the above

6. God's promise of salvation is to be taken ________.
   a. As a divine affirmation, and since God changes, so will its outcome
   b. As an unambiguous affirmation that He will finish what He started
   c. As a promise that finds fulfillment ultimately in the quality of our actions
   d. As a vacillating, somewhat obscure promise that is neither here nor there

7. What is the ultimate source of a Christian's full assurance? ________
   a. When other believers confirm him or her in the faith
   b. Being an ordained cleric in the church of Jesus Christ
   c. The inner testimony of the Spirit conjoined with Holy Writ
   d. His or her success (financial, social, etc.) in society

BIBLE STUDY

1. The believer's quickening by the Holy Spirit is often spoken of in terms of resurrection—being brought from death into life. Being born again, as well as the final resurrection of the dead at the Last Day, both share the same foundation. What is it? Read 1 Corinthians 15:20–23. What imagery does the word *firstfruits* evoke? What will be harvested? What does this say about our unity with Christ Jesus? Continue with Colossians 1:15, 18. What does it share in common with the above passage? What aspect of our unity with Jesus is more deeply communicated in this passage (v. 18a)?

2. Read Hebrews 2:1–11. Re-read verses 2–3a. What does every sin deserve? Is the "if" of verse 3a hypothetical? Why? Re-read verses 5–8 (cf. Ps. 8:4–6). What is the author's point in quoting the Psalms? How does this notion support Jesus' claim in John 10:28? Re-read verses 9–10. Through what did Christ Jesus become the pioneer of our salvation? Who is the "everyone" of verse 9 (cf. John 12:32)?

3. Re-read Hebrews 2:11. The "sanctify-er" and the "sanctify-ees" share what in common? If Christ Jesus is our brother, who is our Father? Describe in your own words the contours of this relationship. Do you know who you are? What does any of this have to do with being fully assured of salvation?

DISCUSSION QUESTIONS

1. Discuss as a group what effects this fellowship, or union, has (or should have) on both our physical and spiritual lives, with regards to 1) its giving us meaning and hope 2) conducting holy lives 3) our church life.
2. Read Romans 8:23 and compare it with 8:12–17. In your own words, explain these passages as they relate to the "already/not yet" paradigm of the Christian life. Read Romans 5:5. How do all of these passages contribute to our understanding of being loved by the Holy Spirit?
3. Read 2 Corinthians 13:14. Is the communion, or fellowship, that which the Spirit creates or that which the Spirit is partner to? Could it be both? Discuss this in light of our discussion on assurance and how we should be seeking to be saturated with the Spirit, so as to experience true peace, or true communion (and therefore true assurance), with the living God.
4. How do the sacraments of baptism and Communion work to assure us of God's salvation?

SUGGESTED READING FOR FURTHER STUDY

Ferguson, Sinclair. *The Holy Spirit*
Gerstner, John. *The ABC's of Assurance*
Goodwin, Thomas. "The Work of the Holy Spirit in Our Salvation," *The Works of Thomas Goodwin*. vol. 6, Tanski Publications